T0375181

Over A Cup Of Coffee

By: W. Y. Lee

authorHOUSE®

AuthorHouse™ LLC
1663 Liberty Drive
Bloomington, IN 47403
www.authorhouse.com
Phone: 1-800-839-8640

Published by AuthorHouse   07/10/2013

ISBN: 978-1-4817-7210-5 (sc)
ISBN: 978-1-4817-7209-9 (hc)
ISBN: 978-1-4817-7211-2 (e)

Library of Congress Control Number: 2013911760

I wish to dedicate my book of poetry to my parents, family and friends who have inspired me to write.

Contents

Contents

Over A Cup of Coffee

Over a cup of coffee brewed
Decaffeinated,
We mulled over our daily woes,
Maternal exchanges, others misunderstood;
By the glass counter,
A myriad of homemade sweet pastries and rolls,
Tempting, to soothe our minds,
Oozing in the air,
The flavours lingering,
Mingling with our voices,
We pause, a temptation,
Questioning the calories,
Seemingly harmful for our mature bodies,
Changing ever more!
Do we really mind, we care?
What havoc, a concern for some
To exercise,
Not yet burdened, a warning,
Signaling in advance, a restriction,
Placed upon us so soon.
A refill?
The waitress asks.

In the midst of our conversation,
We do not mind a brief stop,
Interrupting our train of thoughts,
Thinking about the need
To clear our minds, incomprehensible,
Sipping another cup of cappuccino,
Frothy and creamy to the brim.

Sitting to the right of us,
Another woman

In business attire,
Alone,
Her mind seems so distant,
Drifting towards the window sill,
Waiting
And cooling down her cup of green Matcha tea,
So obvious of her slim body,
Her microwaved warmed, Low fat Blueberry Bran arrived,
She quickly swallowed the broken pieces,
Checked her Iphone,
Mesmerized,
Out of the door,
She left Wearing down her heels.

Another hour
Ending our brief stop,
Exchanging our thoughts, now released,
A discussion, soon forgotten,
A maternal dialogue, all so familiar,
To those who understood
The level of stress.

Small wonders,
We often questioned,
We may share,
Unleashed.
Thinking how much our female companion,
Wagging her tail,
Lying on cemented ground,
Glancing up with her large brown eyes,
She often heard, Listening and patiently,
Not even a whimper,
Sensing, she cares about two companions,
Sharing another day
Over a cup of coffee.

Going Crazy over Food

If I had a moment
Going crazy for food,
Though not seriously
Required,
I pause for a moment,
Listen to my inner voice,
Hearing my mentor
Lecturing us,
Be mindful
Of what we eat,
When we eat,
How much we
Should eat,
Where we eat,
Then,
In my desperation
I changed my mind
And
Think of everything
Except food,
To do something else,
I should take a walk,
Just breathe in and out
To clear my mind,
Dropping by a yoga or
Fitness centre,
Exercise for ten minutes
On a mat or treadmill,
Run up and down the staircase
At home,
Take a shower,
Even if I had taken one already,
Email a friend,

Reach for a glass
Of water
To quench my thirst
And hunger pains,
Google a new message,
Call a friend or relative,
Read a book
Or magazine
Write a poem,
Throw in a load of wash,
Go to a movie,
Listen to music,
Stand in line
For a mid afternoon play,
Turn on the radio
To hear a classical
Bach or Beethoven,
Go window shopping
At the mall,
Walk my dog,
Tidy up my garden,
Water my tropical plants,
Etched another painting,
Go to use another hour
Of my gym membership,
Visit a salon
To cut my hair,
Long overdue,
Volunteer another
Four hours a month,
Meditate,
Think of something
To cheer someone
Out the blue,
Be kind to someone,

Ask to help
Someone in need,
Think for a moment
Of those starving somewhere
On this planet,
I feel so guilty
Just need to change
A long condition,
A habit to unlearn
Over the years,
Steeped with rules
Of conformity,
Culturally, superstitiously,
Thinking how wasteful
To leave something behind,
To avoid that
Crazy urge
To consume
Not healthy for my body
Or mind,
After a change,
I do feel better
To overcome an obstacle
To eat too much,
Giving myself
A positive permission
To override,
Empowering myself
To stay healthy,
Rewarding myself
With self esteem,
As no one else
Can take care
Or know
Our bodies better than
Ourselves.

Out for Lunch

Out for lunch
A rare occasion
To spend an hour
Or less,
Perhaps,
Something to do
Left on the desk
From the client
Or the boss
Time out,
The wait
Was not
To be compromised.
Down to the coffee machine
Entered some change
Into the slot,
Regular, decaffeinated
Or cocoa,
Selected,
Oozed the dark liquid
From the machine,
Nearby,
Sugar packages,
Pink and blue ones,
Artificial,
Or yellow
Denoting similar
In sweetness,
Sprinkling a few

Mixed with powdered
Milk or a carton of cream,
Slurping the surface
Too hot for a moment,
Entered another machine,
A bag of salty chips,
And another,
A tuna sandwich wrapped
In cellophane,
No time to waste,
Deadline pending
In a hurry,
Another hour
The boss had
A meeting
Outside the office
One hour later
At a nearby
Restaurant,
Dining on white linen,
Fresh roses in a vase,
Tableware set
Appropriately,
Over a plate
Of mixed salad,
Crab and shrimp cakes,
He ate,
While listening to
His client

By invitation,
His plate,
Wrapped roll
Of tuna sushi
With strips of
Carrots and cukes,
Blended with sauce,
Each of the men
Had a cup of
Coffee,
One only, thoroughly black,
While the other,
Fresh cream with
Brown organic sugar,
Their conversations
Seemed
Enlightened,
Animated,
Interspersed
With tech usage
Unfamiliar language
Named for equipment
Foreign to others,
Oblivious to others.
Among the who's
Sitting nearby,
The music is
Softly playing,
A quartet of ladies,
Dressed in suits,

Hair coiffed,
Messaged faces,
Bubbles and jewels,
Polished nails,
Stylish shoes,
Or another set
Of men
In business attire,
Sharing an entrepreneurial
Scheme,
The two men
Glanced at their watches
Ready for the
Scheduled meeting
At the office
Where the junior assistant
Set out the papers
For discussion,
He quickly
Tossed the half eaten
Sandwich
Into the steel mesh
Bin,
He finished the
Bag of chips,
Down the last
Drop of coffee,
He was waiting
Patiently,
At the boardroom

For the two men
In discussion
Of a project
Yet to be done
And
Finalized,
Pending
On the outcome
Of the agreement
In writing,
Not a sealed deal
Until the signatures
Were
On the dotted lines,
Out for lunch
More
An in for lunch
Scrambling
To complete an assignment
Without hesitation
Leaving little time
For
Out of lunch.

The Food Stand

Outside,
Open for business,
Next to a roadside,
There stood a stand.
Each dawn,
The Old Woman
Collected woven baskets
Of ripened hothouse
Red tomatoes,
Sweet and juicy,
And
Vine grown, organic fresh,
Long English green cucumbers
From steam filtered green house.
The Old Woman
Sorted each fresh product
In corrugated containers
On display
To sell to passerbys
Or neighbours from the
Same vicinity.
The price by weight
She weighed on
Toledo brass scales
And charged her customers
A reasonable cost,
So envied at stores,
Wholesale farm priced
To make her day
A worthy contribution
Of savings,

She collected
Into a metal can,
She splurged on birthdays
And seasonal celebrations.
By the end of the day
Just before dusk,
She swept her food stand
From daily dust
To end another day,
Closed.

A Conversation on Social Media

A few moments
I pause
Thinking of a conversation
On Social Media,
An invasion of privacy
On the Internet,
Assuming
With a positive attitude
Connecting
With whomever we desire,
Be someone
From our past,
A relative
Or friend.
Seldom seen,
Or once linked
In the past,
An old classmate,
Or someone,
Forgotten
To say sorry,
A wrong
Insignificant
At the time,
It may seem
To someone,
Perhaps,
In a rush,
A gesture of thanks
Should be reciprocated,
Later, better
Than never,
Others may not

Be offended,
Certainly,
Some would
With sincerity,
Some acts
Of kindness
Are expected,
Human nature
Defines who
You are,
Social graces
At home
Or public,
Regardless
Of circumstances,
Rudeness is
Never tolerated,
Or a stranger,
Searching similar,
In agreement
Posting concerns,
Over the years,
Thinking
Out of poverty,
Knowing
Something good
Had happened,
Social Media
Has made
A difference,
Worldwide,
To be connected,
A discovery,
An awareness
To join others
Of similar kind,
A craft perhaps,
Some political thought,

A medical fact,
Maybe a fad,
Scientific or
Environmental
Concerns,
A name unknown,
Jointly followed
For a reason,
Maybe,
Popular
By many
Who may follow
Like birds flocking
In unison
To a designation,
Or a promotion
Of a product
To be considered,
A link
With every conceivable
Imagination,
Making
Introverted
Into extroverted
Without anyone
Knowing
Inside the confines
Of a space,
Just a remark
Replied,
No gesture
Or facial expression,
No intonation,
Monotone derivative.
Incognito
To a printed response,
No identification.
Someone may

Have followed,
Be it on
Facebook, Twitter
Or Pinterest,
YouTube,
And others
On the website,
Blogging, seeking
Some exchange
Of a statement
Or image sent
Through the channels
Instantly,
Mobilizing others
To respond
To the same printed
Matter of concern.
We do fear,
Sometimes
With junk mail
Bugging the system,
Losing data
Unrecovered,
Social media
Inadvertently.
Damaging a reputation
Or interpreted
As cyber bullying
Wasting lives,
Debilitating
With cruel intentions
Unforgiving,
Lowliest cretins,
Absent of facial
Recognition,
Sitting in a
Comfort zone,
Signifying a threat

Manipulating
One's minds
Driving others
To insanity,
Or those
With investigation,
Searching inconceivable
Files
To render
An impasse
Stripped without redemption
Into punitive damages,
A conceived idea
Inviting others to join
Legitimately,
With thousands or
Millions of others
To correct an injustice
En masse,
A simple click,
The message is
Diverted
To the source
Collected
For promotion,
Or join others
To view a video
Gone viral,
Adorable cute,
Or an image
Ominous,
Disconcerting,
Regardless,
Social Media
Is
A concern.

Inside a Chinese Pastry Shop

Passing by the
Pastry shop,
The woman, dressed
In crinkled frock
White apron tied
With a bow behind,
Wearing black patina
Shoes with a dusting
Of white flour,
Her black hair tucked behind,
Her slender fingers
Covered slightly with
A film of
Creamy butter and sugar,
Which stirred my
Hunger pains
Spanning my eyes
Across the array
Of baked goods.
The mixed aromas
Lingering,
Motioned me
From the clear
Ammonia, newsprint
Cleaned
Windows,
To enter,
Inside,
I gravitate

18

To the assortment
On display,
Sugary flaky
Round donuts,
Which melted my mouth
Upon each bites,
Lard, sugar frosted
Almond cookies.
Adjacent
To a mound
Of quarter sized thin
Crispy brown cookies,
Fittingly small
To fill a child's mouth,
Napoleon bars
Filled with
Layers of thinly
Phyllo pastries and
Sweet custards
And fine icing sugar.
The pies were placed
Into a bell shaped
Three layered glass dome,
First layer,
The best flaky
Macintosh Apple pie,
With the cinnamon
Sugar oozing through
The egg coated
Sweet crust,
The second layer,

Banana cream pie
Layered with
Whipped cream
And sweet custard
And slices of bananas
With strands of
Roasted sweet coconuts,
Piled on high, while
The top layer,
Crowned the high
Peaked Lemon Meringue
Pie, thickly filled
With sweet lemon
Filling, made from
Florida flown
Fresh sweet lemons
Squeezed into juice,
Boiled with starch
And tapioca, thickened
And sweetened,
Beneath
A pile of Jersey thick
Whipped cream and
A sprinkling of
Sweet roasted coconut,
Meringue.
At the other side,
A moveable sliding
Window remained open
To see the row of
Nin Go

Nestled on Pyrex
Round Plates,
Ready for the lunar
Celebration,
I watched
The women
Standing around
The round wooden table
Kneading the dough
Moving back and forth,
Adding sprinkling
Of water
Into the batter
Of rice flour and brown sugar,
Proportionately by the
Feel of hands, stretching
And kneading
Placing each mound
In each plate
To be steamed into
Perfection,
A gooey thick
Texture,
Seemingly made,
Symbolically,
Annually
Titillating,
To serve
The palates of those
Who favour
The delicacy

Of
Nin Go.
On the other side,
The same woman
Suggested
More baked goods
On the other side,
She reached out
With flat trays
Of freshly made
Buns or "Bau",
Huge and warm,
Filled with sweet
Rose water coconut
Filled buns,
Black sweet sesame or
Sweet blended red beans
And other buns
Filled with
Barbecue pork, "char shew"
Chicken mixed with onions, and
Some mixed with ham
And free range eggs, and
Vegetarian buns made with
Minced spinach or
Sweet cabbages,
I had a quarter to spend
Enough to buy
Two hot pork buns and
A brown paper bag
Filled with

Small round cookies
And then,
Left the pastry
Shop, closing the door
The sounds
Of clanging cow bells
Trailing behind me.

Kobe

In an unfurnished room
Among crates of boxes,
Except for an old TV,
Still cabled,
I turned on and listened
To an unfamiliar broadcast.
I listened to the sweet melodic voice
Of a west coast singer
Hauntingly piercing my heart
As photos of Animals,
God's creatures,
Inadvertently,
Displayed on screen
I watched in pain and disgust
Etched on these animals,
An inhumane justice
Of abuse and neglect,
I found missing facial expressions,
Some without eyes, window of souls,
Or ears to listen for sounds of direction, Broken bones to deter a
normal pursuit, And worse, absence of Love and care.
The words, repeated
Resonating
A plea,
In search of a caring home
With warm hearts
Yearning some protection
From wicked cruelty.
My bewildered mind
Seemed futile,
Provokingly,
Unless I take action
Requesting,
To adopt,
Arresting

An insane madness.
What an opportune time
I went to the shelter
To search among the maimed
Four or three legged friends
To adopt
I felt like dancing in the air
Looking through inauspicious cages,
I found Kobe,
Loyal and compassionate,
My Golden Retriever,
Light blond ball of fur
Not quite a year old but
Beaten by hellish hands,
Abandoned.
I felt abhorred,
I locked eyes with my companion
Whose eyes seemed so lost in pain?
I caressed his face
And held his small quivering body, so
Assuredly,
I will care forever
As I am in need of a friend
Who answered my plight?
Of concern,
We understood,
Simultaneously,
We need one another
To survive
And love
Unconditionally,
On this earthy planet.

Bad Habits

Bad habits
We often encounter
Daily
Are we less human?
When confronted
By those we assume
Know the etiquette,
The social graces
Or the rules
Public or private,
Or the ethics,
A thin line
Of choosing
Or doing
The right
Or wrong
Under certain circumstances,
Are we to accept?
Or dismiss
An issue
To avoid
A confrontation
And
Is it really
None of our
Business?
As children
We were taught
To say
Our thank you's
And please's
In almost
All Cultures,
Seemingly expected,

Are we
Obliged and
Prepare
To accept,
When someone
Displayed some
Bad Habits,
Intolerable
To digest
In our minds,
Deemed
Unacceptable
By any standard.
What we do wrong
Are we supposed
To apologize
Or be sorry,
Are we
To tolerate
Or empathize
When
Someone
Do the Contrary.
What rules?
Do we follow?
To be
Socially
Accepted,
We choose
To live
And
Endure
To exist,
Regardless
Of
Who we are:

We gave
A Child
Something,
The Child
Refused
To acknowledge
Your offer,
We asked,
What did?
The Child's parent
Taught the Child,
No manners,
No excuses,
No explanation,
Are we to assume
The Child,
Shy or
Rude,
Others
Would argue,
Why bothered?
Who asked?
Us
To give
Generously?
Are we expected
To be acknowledged?
Never minded.
We walked
Away,
Shaking our heads,
We refrained
To teach
The Child.
The same Child
Became

An Adult.
Bad habits
We encountered
Daily
Exist
To annoy
A vicious cycle!
The Adult
Thankless
Have you ever
Noticed
Walking to the door,
Someone
Decided to push
You
In order
To get to the door
Before you do,
Slam the door
In front of you?
Sitting in your vehicle
At an intersection
Waiting for the lights
To change,
Someone revering
The engines
To speed past you
On the right side
Almost damaging your vehicle
Or give someone
A heart attack
Or stroke?
Have you ever noticed
What others do
While waiting for the
Lights to change,

Oblivious to others,
The driver
Is texting on
His or her cell phone,
Or picking noses,
Combing hair,
Putting on makeup,
Cleaning nails,
Brushing teeth.
Gobbling up a sandwich,
Eating leftovers,
Drinking from a bottle,
Reading the newspapers,
Working on assignments,
Smoking or
Littering on the streets.
That same adult
Standing on the street corner
Waiting with a scraper
And bottle
Annoying drivers
Expecting coins
To feed their drug habits
Never realizing
Their daily loot
Added more than one's paycheque
At the end of the day.
Timing
On schedule
Never realizing
Time had lapsed,
Lateness,
Not tolerated,
Rudeness,
Others would assume,
Offended,

At times,
Regardness,
Not realized,
Others
Loathe
Your attitude
Oblivious
To circumstances,
Never excused,
As customed
To timing
And
Schedules.
According
To time,
Nor understood,
As at times,
Interrupted
Being tardy
Ruined relationship,
A respite
Only few
Would forgive,
Give an hour
In advance
To avoid a
Minute
Of tardiness.
On the road
Drivers raced
Through red lights,
Oblivious to traffic rules,
Never a thought
To other's security,
Revering engines,
Passing on the right

Or cutting in,
Barely crashing in
To another's vehicle,
Drivers
Who drink
And drive,
Over the limit,
Endangered
The lives of those
Who may expect
Someone
Never alive
Or maimed
Forever.
We often
Heard
Profanities
Of the lowliest
Kind,
Swearing, cursing
Outrageously,
All the body
Languages
In every culture
Though we would
Not be understood,
Nevertheless,
The gestures
Would said it
All,
Whatever expression
To relieve an inner stress
If directed
To the person
Implied,
Considered

Not a rudeness,
But a disrespectful
Utterance
Never to be
Tolerated or
Empathized.
Invasion of privacy
Break and enter,
A criminal act
Destroyed
By those whose
Habitual bad habits
Ruined the harmony,
Of those
Whose homes
Deemed sacred,
Private and personal,
Never should
An intruder
Has the right
To destroy, steal
Or ruin
Another's home, vehicle
Or personals,
A crime
Not to be
Tolerated.
Public facilities
A common usage
We often find
Washrooms
Left unkempt
By users
With little care
For others
Or those

Whose jobs
To clean
At allotted time,
Shame on those
Who could not
Handle their own mess
Or
Who leave without
Washing their hands
Contaminating
Door knobs
And fixtures,
Shamefully demonstrated
Exiting
Without concern
For sanitary conditions.
Litter,
An exercise,
Often demonstrated
In public places,
A drop of litter
From
Vehicles' windows,
A miss from bins
Set aside,
Strewn all over
Sidewalks, parks
And streets,
We often questioned
The lack of concern,
Young and old.
In lakes, rivers and oceans,
We often found
Litter of sorts,
An environmental concern,
We have often

Stressed,
A rampant neglect
And responsibility,
Dismissed by
Careless cretins.
Are we humanly
Possible to endure,
Accept bad habits,
Tolerate
Just because
Others do,
Or should we deem
Bad habit
None of our business
And
Let the world be,
Assuming
We understood
The trends
Of our present
World.

Bitzy

Found
In sheltered shop
Against the window pane,
Large and wide
In barbed cages
Among other animals
Yelping and meowing
A symphony of sounds,
Bitzy,
Shih Tsu,
Emperor's delight
So tiny and furry,
Oblivious to all,
Her innocent brown eyes
Caught my attention,
Cuddled,
Yearning this owner
To adopt.
I stood there
For a moment
Hesitantly,
I entered,
The ringing of cow bells
Alerted
Two smiling spinsters,
Dressed with aprons
Paw prints designed,
Greeted me warmly,
Standing by the counter,
Sparsely decorated
With colourful tinsels and bells
And a sign which read,

"Animals for adoption,
Donations accepted
Adopt a Pet
If you care."

Any donations would suffice
Rescuing a plight
Of dispair,
My eyes seemed fixated,
Towards a small ball
Of fur,
Champagne colour,
Shiny and soft
Shivering eying me,
Her dark black muzzle
Covering her mouth,
Destiny perhaps,
I held her in my palms,
Soft and cuddly
Irresistible companion,
A lady's best friend,
A love to share,
Forever.

The Blue Porcelain Bowl

Inside my mother's room,
Chantilly lace creamy white
Covering the walls and ceiling,
The bright crystal chandelier
Hung majestically overhead,
Capturing the sunshine glow
From the squared wooden windows
Shining in at dawn,
A gentle westerly breeze
Caressing soft laced curtains,
I watched my mother undress
Her crimson red silk gown,
In front of the mirror
Queen Anne style,
Long and oval sitting
On shiny dark hardwood floor
Next to a cherry wood table where
I found a blue porcelain bowl
Round and translucent
With intricate dragons
And phoenix designs
With significant splendour
Lying next to an ox bone comb,
A soft cotton facecloth,
And a crystal cut bottle
Of sweet French perfume,
Lightly used, so treasured
From distant land
Over ocean wide

And a *Mont Blanc* fountain pen
Lain on a pile of rice paper,
Plainly to see and write
A few verses
To celebrate a new life
On foreign soil.

If You Had A Moment

If you had a moment
What would you say?

I love my earthly planet,

I love God's creations,
His set plans
Through mankind,

I love my parents,
Mother and Father,

I love my family
Connected
From all sides,

I love my children
For whom they are,
Unconditionally,

I love my friends,
Young and Old,
With integrity,

I love Nature
Its beauty
Encompassing,

I love People,
From all walks of life,
Multiculturally,

I love Places
I have lived
And travelled,

I love Food
From all cultures
Fused,

I love Sports,
Seasonal playing
Engaging others,

I love to chat
To learn and listen
From others,

I love to take
A break,
Coffee or tea,
Sipping for a moment,

I love to communicate
By email, letters
Or phone,

I love Art
In all forms
And medium,
Creative,

I love Peace
For all Mankind
Stopping

Wars
For a moment
Of Freedom,

I love the Sun,
Moons and stars,
A galaxy
Of awe,

If I had a moment
To give
A clear direction
Without hesitation
From wrong to
Right,
From false to truth,
From lack of trust
To integrity,
From hate
To love,

If you had a moment,
What would you do?

Art for Art

I stood
Inside the art gallery
In wonder
The display of artwork
Over centuries
The professional artists
Enlightened times
With strokes of paints,
In ancient oils
Or
Watercolours,
Depicted
On canvas,
Stained glass,
Etched,
Historical designed,
In awe,
Countless hours
Of perfection
The lines,
Contours,
Finely defined
Of nobility.
Idyllic
Background
So carefree,
Detailed costumes
As Rembrant's
Portraits, or the
Flesh and nudity
Expressed
Of women
And men,
The cherubic children,
Pastoral playground,

Overflowing
Colours, styles
Adorned,
Detailed
The era
Classical,
Romantic,
Or
Renaissance
Periods
Of past years
In focus
For the naked
Visions
Of those
Standing
Examining
The minds
Of the artists
Neurotic
In ecstasy
Hypnotic
To the naked eyed,
Or in view
Of modern painters
Or sculptors
Using minds
And matter
To produce
Or construct
Meanings
Through their souls
For interpretation,
Our imagination,
Soul searching
Through every stroke
Before us,

Picasso,
Matisse,
Van Gogh,
To name a few,
Whom
We question
Psychologically,
Defining their
State of minds,
Intelligently
Crafted to
Perfection,
The works
Of Emily
Carr,
The famed
Group of Seven,
The landscapes,
Acrylically
Demonstrated,
The modern artists,
The vibrant
Colours,
In depth,
Penetrating
Visuals,
The sculptures
In forms
Of metals.
Defined
Polished
To perfection
Of each era,
Of stones and
Wood,
Chiseled,
Carved, weaved,

By indigenous
First Nations
Over
Centuries,
Authenticated
Treasures
Travelled
With explorers
Or immigrants
Afar,
Asia, Europe,
Scandinavia
Stored
In displays,
On another floor,
A darkroom
Lighted a screen
Depicted
Silently,
Figures
In black and white,
Another,
A stage
For modern artists
Loomed wide
And high,
Structures,
Loose strings,
Sheets of metal,
Boxes, furniture,
Wheels,
An entanglement,
Made a statement
We assumed
Of art form
As transcended
Accepted or rejected,

The curators
With best of intention
Displayed
To all whose
Inquisitive minds
Lured their presence
To view, adjudicate
And assess.
To many,
Art is Art.

Priorities Of A Woman

I sat quietly on the Canada Line
Observing the passengers
Boarding off and on
I noticed a woman
Standing holding a bag
Of groceries
The men sitting
In their blue seats
Glanced at her
Mousey brown hair
Her cowl neck beige
Cashmere
Open,
Revealed her cleavage
The train winded
Her way
Underground
Shuffling along
The tracks.
The men remained
Complacent
Stuck to their seats
Until they reached
Their destination
A lemon rolled off
Her cotton bag
She bent down
Observing
The lemon rolled
Off
Between the legs
Of two men,
One glanced down
Oblivious to the

Fallen citrus
As he scanned
The daily news
The other one
Started rubbing
His nostrils
She stood still
Holding her bag
While her cell phone
Rang
The men glanced
Thinking it was
Their rings,
Similar tones
They heard
One dressed
In business pinstripe
Light grey and black
His black Florsheim shoes
Polished
His partner
Sitting on the same chair
Still reading
The same papers
Now crumpled
Indiscriminately
Over the pages
Until he shifted
To the sports page
The other man
Glanced down
At his Swiss Army watch,
Bulky with gadgets
Ignored her
Avoided her loose fruit
Until the next stop,

The well dressed one exited
Through the wide doors,
The other one sat still
Pulled his black knapsack
Over the empty seat
The woman still stood
Holding the bar
Turned her back,
The man farted
The woman walked away
Left the lemon
Under the seats
Where the two men sat
The next stop
The woman
Dressed in the floral sundress
And weaved tan sandals
Carried her bag
Exited.

Along Spanish Banks

Along Spanish Banks
Ripples of waves
Rolling over the sands
Pebbles and driftwoods,
Midway deeper in distance
Freighters temporary moored
Between north and south
More to the west,
Silhouetted buildings
Dotted the skyline
Below the majestic mountains
Snow capped beyond,
Joggers, walkers
Pacing along the earthy paths,
Dogs unleashed
Roaming freely,
Children,
Running wild against the breeze,
Dipping their feet
Into the wet sands
While the tides are
Still low
Extended the shoreline,
Gently infused with
The Spring air,
Rows of vehicles
Filled the spaces
Of the parking lot,
Nearby.

Beachcombers
Set up nets,
Playing volleyballs
Digging into the sands
Exchanging the throws,
A few early sunbathers
Stretched on thin mats
Absorbing the early
Rays of sunshine,
A couple of elderly folks,
Sitting on a bench
One chatting
the other, oblivious,
Engrossed, reading
A paperback,
Up in the air,
Two kites seemed
Freely floating,
Seagulls, carefree,
Flying swiftly
Over the calm waters,
The concession stands
Open for business,
The smell of food,
Lingered in the air,
The litter
Of leftover wrappers
Added to the grounds
In a short time
By unconcerned polluters,

Not thinking of others,
Bikers and strollers
Intermingled
Crossing paths,
From dawn to dusk,
The landscape
Fused with the sunset
Slowly setting,
Clouds drifting
Seemed darker,
As the waters
Turned to higher tides,
Mothers cradling
Small babies
In their arms,
More tightly
Against a cooler breeze,
The waves
Swished stronger,
As the sun sets
Nature's beauties
Works wonder
Another day.

The Art of Fishing

The art of fishing
A tactful skill
With patience,
I watched
My father
Early before dawn.
Headed out with
His next door neighbour
In his green Ford truck
To catch the
First wave of fish
Squirming by,
High tides
The moon determines,
The night before
Armed with fishing
Gears and tackles,
Selecting colourful
Lures,
Bright and shiny,
Wearing checkered
Flannel shirts,
Red and black
And many pocketed vest
And
Heavy cotton
Champagne coloured
Fishing hats,
Black rubber gumboots,
Pails of sorts
Lined along the rocky pier
The wooden plank
Extended far into the
Cool morning waters,
The moon shining still,

They dangled their rods
Waiting for the catch,
Sizes they knew by heart,
Varied kinds of fish
They decided,
My father's favourite,
Rock Cods
Large eyes, shimmering skins,
Dark ribbed scales,
Plenty to catch,
A delicacy to steam,
Drenched with hot oil,
Soya, ginger and garlic
And green onions
Or black bean sauce,
A fibre
A delightful compliment
Or fried with
Sweet and sour,
And sweet onions,
Pineapples chunks,
Red and green peppers,
Lavished with blended sauce,
Coated with
A soft crispy batter, staying
Silky white flesh
A pile of hooligans,
Slimy,slippery,
Elongated slender fish,
A delicacy
He pickled each year
The two cajoled
Sharing a common pleasure.
Uncommon language
Was no concern
But the art
Of fishing
Was a passion,
They both nodded

With approval and
Satisfaction,
A simple gesture sharing
The same waters
Catching fish,
Knowingly,
Friendships
Endured a lifetime!

Fog

Fog hovering over the city
Mysteriously,
Like a giant Abyssinian gray cat
Stretching miles
Over purplish blue
Mountains and hills
Shrouded within layers
Of rolling clouds,
Drifting through the sky
Enveloped in dense gray
The city lights
Flickered through the darkness
Slowing down the automobiles
Crawling bumper to bumper
On every busy streets
Rushing cautiously
From work, school and home
Walkers and runners,
Some wearing reflectors,
Hesitantly moving
From every directions,
Bikers and motorcyclists
Skirting slowly
Along the traffic
The fog,
A natural phenomena
Created out of droplets,
A veil of secrecy
Within layers of the atmosphere
Dissipating through the air.

Wild Pacific Winds

Wild Pacific Winds
Howling, blowing
Unearthed
Nature's playground
Boughs of fir trees
Cracked, broken
Over trails
Of dirt,
Pine cones, leaves
Scattered
Indiscriminately,
Tattered tarp
Of underbrush
Ransacked, uprooted,
Wavering, shivering
Shady green ferns,
Rows of purplish
White crocuses,
Fields of golden daffodils,
Quivering stately tulips
Ripped, torn
Overnight
Spring's early growth,
Displacing habitats
Of earth species,
Animals and insects,
Scrambling species
Of birds,
An ecosystem
Disturbed
By Nature's call,
Unburdened.
Rolling stones
Running
Along scraps

Of waste
And litter,
A garbage dump,
Left by careless
Planetary cretins.
Wild Pacific Winds
Knocking against
Windows, doors,
Whistling through
Crevices, holes,
Shaking houses
Rumbling over
Cedar, tile
Rooftops,
Shifting, shaking
Earthly ground.
Tossing waves
Under Lion's Gate Bridge,
High against the sea wall,
Pounding the mermaid
At Stanley Park,
Shifting, bobbling
Lighthouses,
Rocking temporary
Overnight freighters.
Lights and banners
Swaying
Over streets and alleys.
In spite of over packed
Shelters,
Homeless vagrants
Huddling under
Layers of blankets
And makeshift boards.
The morning aftermath,
Out of windy chaos,
The winds gyrated

Slowly to a halt,
Leaving a mess,
A touch
Of calmness,
Harmonious,
Overflowing
Nature's realm
Awakening, testing
Those in doubt
Of
Nature's strength.

Hiking about the City

Each day
We plan our routes
Hiking about the city
Trails,
After a year
Of training
Building our strength
Taking walks
An hour a day
At various
Designated areas
Mapped in kilometers
Counting the steps
At Queen Elizabeth Park
Winding
Up to the
Bloedel Conservatory,
Multiplex glass dome,
Down through the
Garden paths,
Bushes
And trees,
Passing by
The rose garden
Along the lower
East end
Of the park
And the tennis courts
Back down

West towards
The lower end
Where children
Crowd around the
Duck ponds,
Around the pitch and putt,
Watching
A couple
Giving each other
Advice
Which direction
To shoot the ball,
Moving along
The winding path,
Southerly
Along the Cambie corridor,
A quarter way,
Almost reaching
The allocated point,
Winding down,
The momentum
Slowing down,
Passing by the Hillcrest
To end our trip
Burning calories
With
Self gratification.

After The Storm

After the storm,
Ruins among rubbles,
Roofs caved in,
Tattered torn ceilings
Cracked cedar shakes,
Broken shattered glass.
Windowless,
Flattened walls,
Doors down,
Destructions destroyed,
Relentless rains,
Hurricanes havoc,
Hollering winds,
Whipping chills,
Graying,
Looming landscapes,
Unearthed mounds,
No heat, no warmth,
No precious water
To drink or bathe,
Possessions lost,
Personals violated,
Heirlooms,
Children's toys, books,
China, furniture,
Clothings
All
Scattered everywhere,
Inconspicuously,
Frightened faces
Futile in despair,
Injured souls,
Maimed,
Lives gone,
Indiscriminately,

Selected,
Drowned in sorrows,
Lost memories,
Precious personals,
Destructively destroyed,
The strength of nature
Never estimated
Power of the Divine,
Violated
In a moment's notice,
Unforgiving
On earth's domain.
Devastation
Out of control
Leaving those
In affliction
In tears,
Hopeless,
Insanely incensed,
Homeless,
Clutching,
Hugging,
Embracing
One another,
Suffering same
The losses
Varying degrees
Of pain,
We pray
For hope
And redemption
For our lack
Of faith
Out of chaos,
Unfathomed turmoils,
Unexpected
To endure,

We must believe,
Soon,
Storm surrenders
We resume
Our daily lives
Anew
After the storm.

Tomorrow after Today

Tomorrow after today
I read your email,
I listen,
Your voice
Quivering
In sadness,
My heart
Palpitating,
Still in silence,
Thoughts of you
In mourning
Of your companion,
In eternity,
Timeless,
A loss so dear,
Memories
Flooding,
Overwhelmingly,
Set in motion
With provoking
Thoughts,
Tomorrow after today,
Recouped,
Exchanges
Of private
Conversations,
Shared
Between
You and the loved.

The many places
Frequented,
Revisited
Seemingly missed,
Operas, films, plays,
Shared,
Music
Familiar
And
Harmoniously
Shared,
Books
Reviewed,
Simple pleasures
Of enjoyment,
The warm
Embraces,
Forever
Caressed
Never forgotten,
From
Dawn to dusk,
Momentarily,
Tears of sadness,
Emptiness,
Memories
Of pain
Endured,
Diminished soon
In time,
The smiles

Of sunshine,
Sweet perfume
Of flowers,
Free flight
Of birds,
Breath of fresh air
Permeating
The environment,
The presence
Lifting
Our hearts
Knowingly,
As those,
In
Immortality,
Close and dear,
Through centuries,
Obligingly,
Accepted,
We witness,
Forever
Reminded,
On our earthly planet,
Life is
Precious,
Few words
To express,
Through
Difficult times,
Would remove
The pain and tears.

You and others,
Enduring,
Moments
Of privacy,
Respectfully
Understood,
Waiting,
Caring
In the wings,
If you need
A friend,
Tomorrow after today.

Peace of Mind

Peace of mind
We seek
For privacy,
After a chore
Of accomplishing
A task,
It matters
Little to others,
We seek
Solace
Inside the church
Every
Sunday,
Our faith restored
Whatever denominations
We may belong,
Peace of mind,
Someone is
In need,
We offer
Out of goodness,
Never
Expected a favour
Back,
A Good Samaritan,
A rare rendezvous
Of encounters,
The memory lingers
An indelible kindness
Etched within
One's heart,
Thoughts of beads,
Precious stones
And gems
From different

Inconspicuous
Areas
Of the world
You sought
With every trip,
Peace of mind,
Thoughts
Of others,
After a long absence,
Without words,
A connection
Lost in eternity,
Never forgotten.

Down At Breakwater

Down at Breakwater
Winding past the marine
Scenic route,
What surpassed beyond
One's mind
Questioning life's dilemma
Shortened too soon,
Others
Do care
Out of concerns
In distress,
At dawn
Decision of strength
The chosen path
Leaving the scars
With no comprehension
The dark waters
Lurking
An invitation
Beyond eternity,
Grey skies
Overhead,
Bleak memories
Faded
That Spring day,
Shrouded,
Deep immersion
Against the rocks
And crevices
Among the seaweeds,
Kelp and barnacles,
Neptune's world
And beyond
The devilish beckoning
You surrender,

Tears shed,
Regrets
Misunderstood
You chose
A world
Without pain
Of bullying,
Too late
For others
Whose burden
Of your memories
Remained constant
Never knowing
How painful
To endure
One's insults,
Unforgettable,
Scarred too long,
Had a moment
To reach your
Tender heart
So sweet and kind,
Oblivious to whom,
Never cared
Enough,
Those
With cruel intentions
Unforgiving
Cretins
Ruined your life
Forever.

On Lulu Island
1950's

Out to the outskirts,
In our green Chrysler car,
Four door, chrome steel,
Black and white tires,
My father drove.
He seemed tireless,
Handling the steering wheels
After an overnight trip
Crossing the Black Ball ferry
Docked at Victoria Harbour,
A short distance
From
Stately Parliament buildings
Or
Across the majestic ivy grown Empress Hotel.
He often mentioned
The big city,
Vancouver, in translation,
Salt Water City,
The waters seemed saltier
Than his Guandong city,
He stepped on the accelerator,
The windows were open,
The winds seemed sharper,
Stepping faster on the pedals,
The car advanced miles out of the city
To open fields,
Flat and below seabed,

74

The buildings of the city seemed
So distant after crossing
The rickety narrow bridge
Into agricultural lands
My father had often reminisced
A familiar homeland.
He pointed
Large tracts of land,
The settlers, though
Presently, mostly Asians
Were
British, or of
European descent,
Lived and toiled
Acres of land.
Their livelihood,
A common bond
Of interest and intrigue
Producing.
Far from the roadsides,
Their distinctive character homes
Set far into the fields.
Just over the bridge
Fresh fruity scent enveloped
The unfamiliar areas,
Sweet blend of perfumes,
Punctuated with fruit trees,
Wild berry bushes,
Sweet corn stalks,
Rows of cabbages and potatoes,
A magnificent sight

Triggered our minds with awe,
Fruit and vegetables stands,
Found along dirt roadsides,
For interested buyers,
Abundant supply of baskets,
Selected to sell
Or, by choice,
Picked our own
Baskets to the brim
From fields and orchards.
Towards the end of
The long stretched road,
The Fraser River ran
Freely flowing,
Along high ditches,
Fishermen with rods
Stood on edges
Patiently waiting a catch.
Along high ditches,
Bogs, dykes, peat moss,
With wild berries, ivy ponds,
Brown rusks and reeds.
A Nature's delight,
Grey white seagulls
Soaring high and low,
Over eagle nests
Hidden within tall evergreens,
Not forgotten
On Lulu Island.

Christmas Rush

Busy shoppers
Scurrying around from
Shops to shops
Searching for one
Special gift for
A special person.
Or parents, siblings
Similar account
Among all shoppers
Crowded like sardines
Packed with shopping bags
Among baby carriages
Angling from all directions
With babies
Crying, screaming or
Sleeping soundly
Undisturbed,
Among the restless,
Mothers dragging toddlers
In and out,
Stopping and pushing
Holding their small hands,
One holding an ice cream cone
Dripping over their faces
Or smearing the clothing
Of those passing by,
Some glancing indignantly
Without hesitation
Or those not mindful
Of anything,
As their minds so
Occupied,
Thinking what to buy,
Unless,

For a moment,
Eyes fixated
On display
An item of intrigue,
They entered
Unquestionably,
To search for sizes
Or colour,
Exacting what was
On the model,
The mother and toddler
Waited
For the clerk
Rummaging through
Hoping to find the
Perfect dimension
For the client,
Those among others
With a slow gait,
Or a cane,
Moving along
Trying to find a gift
For their children's
Children
Among the rows
Of aisles,
For a dress or toy
Unimaginable
Assortment,
The pampered ones
Indeed!
Nearby,
The tech shop
Busier than usual,
Shoppers
Curious

Over new applications,
Added to computers,
I phones, Ipad,
Instrumentation
Enhanced with
Gadgets,
Eyes fixated
Glaring
On the screens
With novelties,
Shifting the mouses
Searching
For something new
Or unusual,
Comparing notes.
Further along,
Passing by
Some shops
Perfuming the air
From various essences
Emanating from
Soaps and oils
On display
Packaged in baskets
On display
Luring those
Who pamper themselves
Constantly,
With creams and lotions
Extending the quality
And texture
Of skins turning
Rough, aged
Into suppleness and
Youth
Hiding blemishes

With products
Of enhancements
Daily and routinely,
Winter gear
Attracting
Skiers and snowboarders
Where equipment
And clothing
Made more
Suitable
To withstand
Temperatures
Above normal use.
At the corner,
Shoes
Ubiquitous
Ranging in styles,
Colours and sizes,
Heels, flats, boots
Or runners,
Then, the toy shop,
To delight any child
With so many toys
Of kinds, models and shapes
For a girl or
A boy,
Inside the noisiest
And biggest
Displays of wonder,
Touch and sounds
Of inventive minds,
Time is running
Conveniently located
From all directions,
A carousel
Of eateries

To attempt weary
Shoppers,
The temptation,
The smells
Wafting the air,
Sweet aromas,
Fried, braised, grilled
To perfection,
Ready to fill
Mouthwatering
Souls,
Weighted with packages,
Tingling, weary feet
Need a rest,
Children and babies
Crying and begging
Trying all methods
Of interruptions
To send a message
Of defiance,
Demanding a temporary
Stop,
Airing in public
A break of
Entitlement,
A rest,
To fill hungry mouths
And to see
A priceless smile,
Innocent and naive,
Of glee and
Contentment
On young faces
Is worth
A Christmas rush
And
Anytime of the year.

The Perfect Holiday Crime

Verse one:
Attempted Break and Enter

Ho! Ho! Ho!
Who is knocking at my door?
Who may I ask?
Knock! Knock! Knock!
Intensely and hard,
I peered into my peephole,
My goodness sake,
It is Santa!
Dressed in his red velvet suit and hat, Carrying a large
black meshed knapsack, Heavy black boots, Wearing
a black beard, His bushy brown eyes Piercing madly
through the hole, I am in doubt, My car broke down,
he shouted, I need your help?
In bewilderment,
Where was his sleigh?
Another strange fellow, dressed
In green outfit and pointed hat,
Came to the back door,
Double bolted and laser set
All windows barred with alarms,
I heard him rattling my doorknob,
My black cuddly Rottweiler is
Growling fiercely,
Beware of Dog,

Could this would be Santa or his Elf
Not read?
Our signs and stickers, designated
Block Watch trained neighbourhood,
All items engraved and marked!
What is he doing at the back?
So suspiciously, I questioned?
No stranger is allowed,
I am warned,
That is no Elf
Or Santa,
I reached for my cell phone,
Call 911,
Never open your door
To strangers,
Uninvited or unknown,
A rule I remember
Each and every day!

Verse 2:
Attempted Theft at the Shopping Mall

At my busy shopping mall,
I parked my silver Honda,
Equipped with red steering bar and
Immobilizer blinking blue,
Wheel locks and gas locks
Secured, empty
Of items,
The only spot left
So dark and distant,
Among packed vehicles
With every make and model,
The sign read four hours,
An allotted time,
I assumed.
Passing by each vehicle,
I observed,
Packages and bags piled
Visible in sight,
A thief's delight.
An opportune moment
To break and vandalize,
I found an unlocked vehicle,
Shiny black Mercedes,
The owner in question
Left behind, without due care,
Forgotten perhaps,
I moved along,
A security guard, wearing
His black uniform with reflective yellow stripes, Riding
through the parking lot, Checking with community Policing
volunteers, Caring souls, Preventing crime, Going to each

vehicle, slipping A warning notice of care, Deemed
insecure, Are these drivers paying attention?
I was almost close to the door,
A whimpering sound startled me,
A child or dog?
A small black curly poodle,
Huddling near the door,
Shivering waiting for his owner,
Does he know he is cold or
Is snatched away?
I motioned the biker
To make a public
Announcement soon
To address the crowd
Of busy shoppers.
Then, I spotted a van,
All windows at the back covered,
Circling slowly around the vehicles,
License plate covered with dirt,
Almost not deciphered,
Two men, eyes fixated
With intent to check,
Some inviting cache perhaps?
I do recall,
Some years ago,
A young woman, just finished work,
Was heading home with her load
Of Christmas bags and coach purse,
Being yanked by a passing van,
She held on tight to her purse,
The strap broke, sending her down
On the ground, her shoulder wounded
She was lucky, others were around,
The van disappeared
Before the police arrived,
A lesson, unsuspected,
Learnt in pain.

I entered the store,
So jam packed with shoppers,
Pushing around,
I wonder again,
Are there thieves among,
Who might snatch my large bag
Or wallet unnoticed,
Or be bear sprayed, another incident,
Reminding me of desperate men
Robbing for jewels, or
Should I be aware that I might see?
A youth stealing goods go unnoticed, either For money,
drugs or greed, Sadly it seems, Ruining mind and body, I
would As all decent citizens should Preventing crime.

Out of the Blue

Out of the Blue
Something happens
Someone is there
Unexpectantly,
Leaving us bewildered
At times
For the best
Or worst
Of times,
Perhaps,
Our lives changing
Momentarily
Before our eyes,
Who knows
Tomorrow
Is a different time
We need
To grasp
The moments
Out of the blue
Like the crystal
Snowflakes
Disappearing
On a wintry ground,
Like hearing
An angelic voice
Now silent
Singing in the heavens
Forever,
Like giving thanks
To a friend
Gone unappreciated,
Like hugging
Our parents

Tightly, securely
Once more,
Like visiting
A place
Never travelled,
Like taking a course
Cancelled,
Like seeing
An architectural monument
Now ruined,
Like a stranger
Helping another stranger
At home
Or abroad,
Like a criminal
Breaking into homes
And vehicles,
Losing privacy
And possessions
Without redemption
Or penalty,
Like eating
A sampling
Of culinary delights,
Our taste linger,
Or capturing
A photo
Of some exotic place
Or someone,
Now a blur
Of memories,
Like slipping
An utterance,
Once said,
Offending
Publicly or privately,
Never quite the same
Even with apologies,

Out of the blue,
Species of nature,
Endangered,
Now extinct,
Like a careless
Mistake,
Drinking
Or driving
Out of limits,
Causing lives,
Extinguished
Like the flames
Of an open fire
Causing destruction
Of wild habitats,
Never recovered,
Out of the blue,
Something
Or someone
We care and love
Gone forever.

Along Kitsilano Beach

Along Kitsilano Beach
Footprints
In
Shades of sands
Shifting
With the waves
Ebbing
Over shells and pebbles,
A child's pail and shovel
Piled underneath
Mounds of makeshift
Sandcastles.
An elderly couple,
Sitting on one wooden bench
Next to abandoned logs
Indiscriminately hauled
Along the beach,
Conversing,
A hard bound romance book
In the old woman's hands,
Aged yet smooth,
As her soft porcelain face
Her wool tartan scarf
Swung around her thin neckline
Draping over tweed wool coat
And pants and black leather boots,
She bought to read,
The old man,
Ruddy complexed,

Wrinkled face,
With a whisper
Of scant whiskers,
Barely noticeable
Under his brown tweed cap
And coat,
As he chatted and
Held his companion's hands,
While holding a cane
In another,
Listening to his complaints,
Making a conversation
Almost inaudible to her ears,
A familiar, unchanged
Monotones,
A wandering unleashed dog
Came by,
Sniffing around the
Parameters where the couple sat
Quietly
Waiting for the
Mandarin orange,
Magenta red sunset
To set
Along Kitsilano beach
Where the two met
Undefined years,
Doing the same
In the twilight days,
Still within their hearts,

Reminiscing
Memories
Of yesterday,
Before they walk
Back to their strata home,
Overlooking the beach,
Spending time
Together.

First Frost

Scantily dressed, shivering in my dressing gown, I glanced
through my cloudy windows Through the green worn shutters,
I shivered and noticed the icy layers of frost, Draping over my
cedar patched roof, Echoing the first sign of winter.

Silver wisps clung lightly over pine,
Sending me scented fragrance in the air, In wonder, I
observe this transient pleasure.
Solitude, unfettered sensations,
Prismatic shaped, transformed crystals, Thinly layering an
unfamiliar film Over my son's finished cut of grass, Mowed
just last week.

I meditate after my yoga lesson
Within the same deteriorating walls,
My mind wanders reminiscing
A foreign singular continent.
Lying unspoiled south of the equator
Where warmth envelopes our bodies.

We met, an endearing friendship blooms.
Two strangers crossing miles away
Sharing an unfamiliar residence,
Where at dawn,
Sweet eucalyptus perfumed the air,
Young toddlers, innocent and carefree,
Like its wild furry marsupials,
Out from magnificent Opera House,
An architectural gem, its acoustics,
Permeate the atmosphere with exquisite sounds, There was
a purpose to uproot, Fulfilling another project with expertise.

The juxtaposition of seasons
In sharp contrast
From different continents,

Sharing the same earthy planet,
Celestial sun and moon,
A similar phenomena,
Remain familiar we know.

First frost slowly dissipates
Into oblivion after the afternoon sun,
Teasing us temporarily,
The chills now subdued,
A brief reverie of glistening wisps
Surrender back to Nature's earthy domain.

Mother's Poem

Dawn is breaking
I listen to the drizzles
Tapping against the window sills,
I am awake thinking about another day
Collecting my thoughts vicariously living Through
those who left my wombs, Thinking how many days
are left before I drift Indeterminately, as all my
ancestors before me Hearing their voices so silently
Yet, so mindful I am repeating the same sweet tunes
Of care and affections, Reminding me daily that
we do things for a reason For basic needs and care,
Times are imminent, Sounds of laughter and cries,
unhindered, Relentlessly, I repeat to accomplish
Simple tasks amid all clutter Of mind and domain,
Listening, empathizing, tolerating, Lost in transitional
exchanges, Restless, I am seemingly being dismissed,
My maternal role, Diminished, An unqualified
maternal instinct Is vacant, Extinguished.

The Morning After

The blaring alarm
Awoke me
I had just fallen asleep
Listening to
Breaking news
Of an earthquake
At Haida Kwaii,
Known as
Queen Charlotte Islands
Along the west
Pacific Coastline
Shaking the Richter's scale
We were forewarned
The Big One
Was imminent
Colliding triple plates
Gyrating beneath
Our grounds below
A disaster
In waiting
To destroy our
Lives and properties
We confront
Man's weakness,
Nature's maddening viles,
Rippling effects
Of our wild oceans
Sending tsunamis
Across the Pacific
To the Hawaiian Islands,
What preparations
Would protect
Our daily needs
For disasters of

Significant dimensions
Sending unfathomly
Shockwaves
Sending shivers
Down our spines
We question our authorities
How to stay safe
From harm of
Nature's violent
Dress rehearsals,
We need our supply
Of precious water
Limited in capacity,
Conserve we must.
Where do we go
When disasters hit us
Out of control?
Each to our own,
Those with expertise
Will aid first
Those in need
Of emergency care,
Our lines of communications
Will be cut off
Until they are restored,
We assume
Seventy two hours
Of personal survival,
We need to know
Where to seek help,
Somewhere,
Are we so informed,
A catchment area,
Are our neighbours accounted?
Perhaps not in
So many words,
As complacency
Overrules

We may drown ourselves
In Bacchus drinks
For all they may care
Not joining our meetings
To learn how to
Stay as a survival unit
In time of emergency,
But those close
In distance,
May assist than wait
For those too distant
To aid immediately,
The sirens sounds
Blaring in the air,
Imagine it was dark
In the middle of the night,
Our slumbers shattered
By a roar or
By ceaseless shakes,
The wild winds
Whipping around our homes,
Breaking our windows,
Objects unsecured,
Rolling off the shelves
Colliding,
Ceilings collapsing,
Our roofs caving in?
Where are my heavy
Boots and shoes,
No bare feet
To walk through the mess?
Sending gusts of winds
Through our open spaces,
We turned ourselves
Into a corner
Covering our faces,
Bodies,
Hanging in,

No lights to turn on,
No clean water,
Contaminated perhaps,
No calls to make,
A deadening silence,
Do we have enough water
To drink or clean,
Do we have a covering,
A blue tarp,
Heavy enough
Now, a shelter
To save from harm
Or sleep,
Are there enough bags
For our waste?
A hammer or crowbar
If we need to escape
From rubbles,
Do we have a portable radio
With unexpired batteries
To listen
We assume
The worst?
Do I have a safety kit,
If I am injured?
Do I have enough food,
Scanning my pantry?
No electricity to cook.
How safe am I,
Questioning how and when
To turn off
The gas meters,
A total shutdown,
Buildings collapsing,
Our streets rippling apart
We are our brothers's keepers
To lend our humane hands
To those in need,

The time may be imminent,
Let us be prepared
In event,
A disaster occurs
On this earthly planet
Where we live
In close harmony
With those we care.

The Wait

I wake up
One morning,
Received
An email
In distress.

A separation
In the works
I questioned
The couple,
Romantically
In love
In perfect harmony,
The reality
Of years
Faded
What happened?
Now estranged
In distance,
The personalities
Become a blur,
Fleeting
Moments
Of wedding bells
Chimed
Resonantly
That hot sultry summer
Afternoon.

The blushing beautiful
Bride
In coiffed hair
With curls flowing,
Tucked neatly

Under the laced,
Patterned veil,
A strand of pearls,
Lined her delicate neck,
The chiffon laced,
White wedding gown
With trailing crystals,
Shining patina white
High heels,
The diamond rings
Glistened
In the sunlight;

The handsome
Groom
Held her soft hands
With polished nails,
His European style
Black tuxedo suit
With matching tie
And starched white
Shirt with gold cuffs inks,
Blended well with
His new gold carat
Ring,
His polished
New Florsheim shoes,
The couple
Winding down the steps
Of the church,
As attendants
And
Guests and relatives
Followed,
Witnessed
An holy reunion;

Happily settled

In a home
It seems,
Years faded,
Busy lives
Entangled,
Differentiated
Patterns
Ensued,
Matters of opinions
And attitudes
Differed
From endless
Degrees
Of incompatibility,
Love,

The once Romantic
Feeling
Seemed so faded
Lost and distant,
Then,
Weathered pain
Of defeat
Came,
The chill
Of agony,
Unfathomed,
Now deflated
To the bottom
Pit,
The other,
Controlled
Resolutely,
Strained
Daily by years
Of defeat,
Avoided
The inevitably

Inner weakness
Of surrender
Cheated,
Unscrupulous
Character in question
In deals,
A liaison
In secrecy,
A destruction
Became
An invasion
Of privacy
Of souls,
Forgiven
With empathy,
Tolerance,
A resiliency
Dauntingly
Accepted.

Over a decade
Of unimaginable
Detente,
Unacceptable
Vocal abuse
Pursued,
Emotional turmoil
Unforgiving,
A prisoner
Chained
Hopeless,
Through the courts.

A mélange
Of rules,
Excuses
Demanded,
Lawyers

In pursuit
Of cases,
Withdrawn,
Voiceless
Opinions
Established
In precedents,
Mounting expenses
Through
Exchanges of
Words,
Meaningless,
When decisions
Handed down,
Defeated
By a single statement:
Unfathomed,
Unacceptable,
The cases
Overturned
Over the years
Ensued,
No positive outcomes.

The woman
Strained
To the limits
Her face,
Once full
Of vitality,
Withdrawn,
Lines etched
In despair,
Hopes faded
Locked
In trials,
Waiting in courts,
Seemed

Out of context.

The slim figure
Faded
Into
A matronly figure,
The slower gait
Pacing awkwardly,
Unrecognizable
Until we met again,
The familiar face
I greeted and hugged
Lingered
In my arms
Not yet changed
Seeing a familiar face,
Tears flowing,
Understood,
Knowing
Others
Do care
And listen,
In thoughts
Of others
With similar
Outcomes
Pending
At courts,
A decision
In waiting,
Yet to be
Resolved.

On the Bus

Sitting on the bus
Just behind a row of chairs
Marked for elderly, handicapped
Or parents with babies
I noticed
With each passing stop,
Someone steps in,
Showed their card,
Or plunk a few coins
Next to the driver,
Cheerfully greeting,
Even if it was a bad morning
Or day or a hangover
Watching a defeat
Of their hockey team
Or spent a day
With some friends
Who got married
Or hitched,
Or sadly,
Leaving a child behind
In a care centre or school,
It did not matter,
It was his job
To be courteous and
On time,
Dawn to sunset,

Checking left and right,
Walking passed me
Quickly, found a seat
Somewhere
Down the aisle,
Then, the clock

Ticked
Unassumingly,
Unstoppable
Seconds,
Whether we like it
Or not,
Scheduled for some
Unless
A disregard
For tardiness,
Time is fixed
For employment.
Rules of the routine
Never change,
Otherwise,
Disordered,
The bus driver,
Seeing a wheelchair
Stepped on the lever
To lower the platform
The woman
Lifted her card
And parked
Herself
Next to the side,
At another stop,
A woman
Cradling her
Crying baby
Lifted her empty buggy,
Showed her bus pass.
And moved to the opposite
Side of the wheelchair
The baby started to cry
Louder,
Passengers glanced,
So accustomed

Of each encounter,
Some ignored,
Others attempted
To distract
The baby,
The cries turned
To coos,
While the bus winds
Through the main streets,

Later,
School's out
Students scrambling
To available seats,
Oblivious to who were sitting
On each side
Occupying the restricted
Row of chairs,
Knapsacks, cellphones,
iPads, iPhones, laptops,
Gadgets hanging
From head to toe,
Giggles, shouts
Rude profanities
Exchanges,
Clothing mixed
Attire,
Grungy, uniformed,
Casual,
Make up smears,
Hairs in disarray,
Not a quiet moment
In escalation,
The baby slept
Through, oblivious
To everything.
Rush hour,

The bus is jam packed,
No space to budge
Like a can of sardines,

Standing room only
Cramped
Next to the wheelchair
And baby cartridge.
The bus jolted
With every stop,
The driver
Continued
His happy disposition
Maneuvering
On designated lanes
Dropping off
Riders
Exiting
Sometimes
With a thank you
Or nothing,
Unappreciated,
Thinking just
Another job,
The driver may
Enjoy his occupation,
Or need to make
A decent living.

Spaces Within Places

Spaces within places
A questionable dilemma
Not knowing
What goes on
Behind doors,
A child,
Left alone,
Unattended
For a few hours
A bottle of milk,
Crumbs of
Arrowroot cookies
As a treat,
Among some plastic
And wooden toys,
A small tv,
Blaring just loudly
Showing cartoons
In the cramped
Room
Used for dining
And cooking,
Just a toddler,
Not yet
Out of diapers,
Left alone
While the guardians
Left
For work,
To earn a few pennies
Supplementing
On scant wages
Until noon,
Little sibling,

Still in grade school,
Comes home
To fix some lunch
Peanut butter jam,
Devilled egg and ham,
Or plain toast
With margarine,
The two siblings
Ate together,
They hugged,
Dishes left behind,
She left,
Locking the door,
The toddler
Nods,
Time for a nap,
Huddling his brown
Teddy bear
On a makeshift
Bed
Lying
On the linoleum floor,
I asked,
My answer,
Short and abrupt.
Commenting,
Need the food
On the table
Or starve,
Our alternatives
To meet
The necessities
Of life,
We make do
For what
We have.
None of my business,

I walked away,
Shaking my head
In bewilderment,
I cautioned myself
They are working
To earn a living
Not on welfare,
Humbly they
Manage and live
Making do,
Minimum care
They do love
The child
Under any circumstances,
Surviving
On meagre wages,
Who are we to question
A family
Living
To exist,
Who need no help
Or are we to support
Thinking we know
What is best
For them,
Sending social assistance,
Strangers
Interrupting their best
Of intentions,
Working with solutions,
Essentials
To make a daily living,
Humble pride,
To avoid
Being unnecessarily
A homeless
Situation.

Over a Teapot of Tea

Over a teapot of tea
Two friends
Conversing,
Reminiscing memories
Of past days,

The fragrance lingers
With every fill
And brew,
Jasmine, Oolong,
Perhaps, Matcha
Roasted leaves,
Grind to perfection,
Selected
From tea terraces
Or
Earl Grey
Steamed with milk
And honey or
Vanilla,
Just plain Black tea,
The favourite
For an early start,
English Breakfast or
Darjeeling,
All blends
So exotic,
Titillating palates,
Healthy,
Though caffeinated,
A balancing act
To stimulate
The mind and body
To start the day

Over a teapot of tea,
Or
At noon,
Sipping teas,
Degreasing, detoxing
Our meals
Layered with grease
And sweetness
Until sunset,
The familiar teapot,
Clay, fine porcelain,
Stainless steel,
Ceramic
Or glass,
It matters little,
The teapot
So well used,
Nourishing our health,
At the end of our dinners,
Two friends,
Animated,
Still conversing,
Sipping teas
Finishing our meals,
Gratified and thankful.